Outdoor Adventures

ROCK CLIMBING

Tatiana Tomljanovic

WEIGL PUBLISHERS INC.

Published by Weigl Publishers Inc.
350 5th Avenue, Suite 3304, PMB 6G
New York, NY 10118-0069

Website: www.weigl.com

Library of Congress Cataloging-in-Publication Data

Tomljanovic, Tatiana.
  Rock climbing / Tatiana Tomljanovic.
     p. cm. -- (Outdoor adventures)
  Includes index.
  ISBN-13: 978-1-59036-667-7 (hard cover : alk. paper)
  ISBN-13: 978-1-59036-668-4 (soft cover : alk. paper)
  1. Rock climbing--Juvenile literature. I. Title.
  GV200.2.T65 2008
  796.522'3--dc22
                                          2006101981

Printed in the United States of America
 2 3 4 5 6 7 8 9 0 11 10 09 08 07

Project Coordinator
Tatiana Tomljanovic

Design
Terry Paulhus

CONTENTS

All About Rock Climbing

Climbing can be an exciting and energizing activity. Some people climb to the tops of mountains. Others climb steep rock formations, such as cliffs and boulders. This type of climbing is called rock climbing.

Rock climbing as a sport began in the late 1800s. It started as a way for mountain climbers to practice their skills. On June 27, 1886, W. P. Haskett-Smith climbed Napes Needle in Great Britain. Napes Needle is 115 feet (35 meters) high. This was the earliest recorded rock climb done for enjoyment.

Today, rock climbing is common among people of all ages and skill levels. People can climb mountains, boulders, or rock cliffs. Although rock climbing requires special equipment and training, anyone can learn. Many climbers learn basic climbing skills at indoor gyms. This is called sport climbing. They practice on **artificial** climbing walls. Then, they can try climbing a real rock face. Rock climbing is a challenging sport for climbers of all skill levels.

Moab, Utah, is a popular destination for advanced rock climbers.

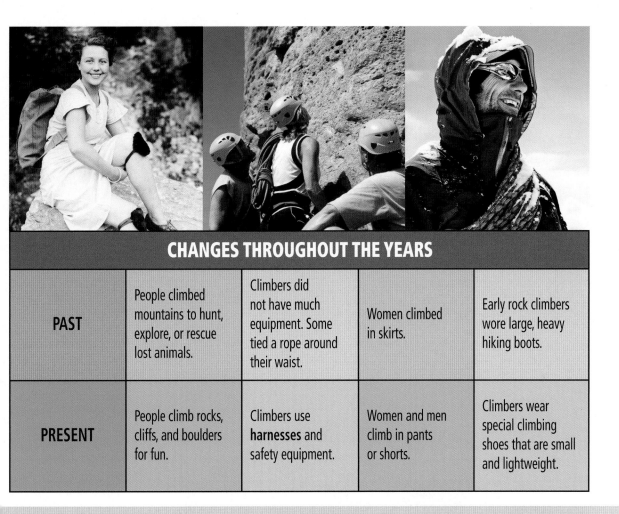

CHANGES THROUGHOUT THE YEARS

PAST	People climbed mountains to hunt, explore, or rescue lost animals.	Climbers did not have much equipment. Some tied a rope around their waist.	Women climbed in skirts.	Early rock climbers wore large, heavy hiking boots.
PRESENT	People climb rocks, cliffs, and boulders for fun.	Climbers use **harnesses** and safety equipment.	Women and men climb in pants or shorts.	Climbers wear special climbing shoes that are small and lightweight.

For a person who weighs 140 pounds (64 kilograms), climbing can burn as many as 700 calories in an hour.

Getting Started

There are many types of rock climbing. Once beginners have tried sport climbing at an indoor gym, they can learn top-roping. Top-roping is done by securely fastening a rope to the top of a climbing surface. This rope holds climbers as they climb.

In traditional, or free, climbing, climbers make their own path up the rock. A pair of climbers is connected by a rope. They climb the rock face while carrying their equipment. As they climb, the climbers place wedges into the rock's surface. They hook their rope to these wedges. If one of the climbers falls, the rope will catch at these points.

Rock climbing can be dangerous. Climbers must have the proper safety equipment. They should also know how to use the equipment properly.

A harness attaches a climber to a rope. The harness is worn around the waist, with loops around each leg.

All the Right Equipment

A helmet is one of the most important pieces of climbing gear. If the climber falls, his or her head is protected. Helmets can also protect climbers from falling rocks.

Climbing shoes are thin and fit snugly. These shoes allow climbers' feet to fit onto very small ledges or inside small cracks in the rock. Each climbing shoe has a rubber sole, heel, and toe that grips the rock and will not slip. The shoes also protect climbers' feet from sharp rock.

Ropes protect climbers during a fall. They can also help climbers return to the ground after a climb. The most common type of climbing rope is the dynamic rope. Dynamic ropes are elastic, or stretchy. During a fall, they will stretch a small amount. This helps **absorb** the impact of the fall and prevents injury.

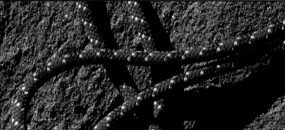

Belay devices stop the climbing rope from moving. This prevents climbers from falling to the ground. There are many types of belay devices. Some of these include the sticht plate, ATC, and the gri gri.

Anchors attach the rope to the rock wall. There are many types of anchors, including chocks, camming units, ball nuts, and bolts.

Carabiners are metal loops with openings that lock. They are used to connect different pieces of climbing equipment, such as belay devices and harnesses.

Rock Climbing Basics

Most people climb in pairs. While one person climbs, the other person belays. One end of the rope is attached to the climber. The other end is attached to the belayer. The belayer threads the rope through a belay device. This allows the belayer to stop the rope from moving with little effort. The belayer will stop the rope if the climber falls or if the climber wants to stop and rest. Once the belayer stops the rope, the climber can let go of the rock and dangle in mid-air.

Climbers may need to rest during their climb. They may become tired. If they reach a difficult area, climbers may need to plan their next move. People who enjoy rock climbing learn how to make it easier. They use handholds and footholds to help them. These are moves that climbers can use to grip or step up as they climb.

Climbing with other people is a good idea. If one climber is badly injured, the others can go find help.

Some basic handholds are jamming, crimping, and pinching. Jamming is shoving fingers, an arm, an elbow, or even a foot into a crack. Climbers use jamming when they need extra grip so they can reach the next hold. Crimping is putting the tips of all fingers on an edge and tucking the thumb over the index finger. The thumb adds strength to this grip because the thumb is the strongest digit. Pinch grips allow climbers to use very small pieces of rock as handholds by pinching them.

get CONNECTED

Learn how to tie climbing knots at www. abc-of-rockclimbing.com. Click on "info" and "techniques & training."

Footholds are more important to climbers than handholds. This is because leg muscles are much stronger than arm muscles. Two common foot moves are edging and smearing. Edging is when climbers stand on small ledges with the inside edge of their feet. When there are no ledges, climbers must smear. Smearing is placing the bottom of a foot on a rock and pushing with the balls of the feet and the toes against the rock.

Smearing helps keep a climber's foot in place.

Rock Climbing Levels

The level of difficulty when climbing a route depends on many factors. Longer routes are harder to climb than shorter routes. If a route does not have many handholds and footholds, the climb will be more challenging. **Vegetation** can make the rock harder to grip. Soft rock types, such as shale, are hard to climb because they break easily. Granite, limestone, sandstone, and gneiss are the most common rock types for climbing. These rocks are very hard. They are less likely to break than other rocks.

The first climbers to **ascend** a new rock climbing **route** give the route a difficulty **rating**. Different parts of the world use different systems of rating. In North America, routes are graded using the Yosemite Decimal System. Each level of difficulty is matched with a decimal rating. These range from 5.0 to 5.15. The decimal system is further divided by letters. Any route graded 5.10 or higher is assigned a letter from "a" to "d." The rating 5.10a is easier than 5.10b.

Finding the right grip can be difficult. Climbers should take the time to make sure they have a firm grip on a secure part of the mountain.

The fabric of a portaledge is supported by a wire frame. The frame hangs by straps from a single point.

get CONNECTED

To learn more about rock climbing rating, visit www.safeclimbing.org/about_overview.htm.

If a climb takes more than one day to finish, climbers may spend the night in a portaledge. This is a shelter that has a nylon floor and a waterproof tent. The portaledge hangs from anchors attached to the rock wall. Inside, climbers can sleep hundreds, or even thousands, of feet above the ground.

YOSEMITE DECIMAL SYSTEM	
SPORTS	5.13–5.15
EXPERTS	5.11–5.12
ADVANCED	5.8–5.10
INTERMEDIATE	5.5–5.7
BEGINNER	5.0–5.4

The Yosemite Decimal System uses numbers to rate the difficulty level of a climb. It is the main rating system in North America.

Staying Safe

Rock climbing is an **extreme sport**. There are many risks. Before beginning a route, climbers need to be prepared. First, they must reach their route safely. Hiking is the only way to reach many climbing routes. To keep from becoming lost on the way, climbers plan their hike in advance. They carry a map and **compass**. Climbers should always tell someone where they are going and when they will return.

Falling snow and ice are a danger when climbing in snow.

It is a good idea for climbers to wear helmets at all times. Climbers can easily be hurt by rocks, ice, dirt, or gear falling from above. When objects fall from above, climbers should press their bodies close to the rock face. This will lessen the chance of being hit by the object. Climbers should always keep their face to the wall. If they look up, they may be hit in the face by a falling object.

It is a good idea to check weather conditions before climbing. Rain or snow can make the rock slippery and hard to hold. Cold weather can cause **hypothermia**. An avalanche takes place when rocks or snow quickly slide down the side of a mountain. A climber could be buried beneath the rocks or snow.

Altitude sickness is a risk when climbing at 8,000 feet (2,400 m) or higher. It is caused by a lack of oxygen in the air. People with altitude sickness often become dizzy. They may have shortness of breath or feel confused. To avoid becoming sick, climbers should spend a day or two at high altitudes before continuing to climb. This will allow their body to adjust. Some mountain climbers carry an oxygen tank. Climbers can breathe oxygen from the tank.

TIP

Most European climbers use two ropes. If one rope fails, the other will support the climber.

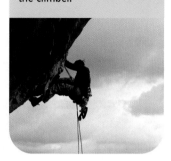

Visit **www.athro.com**. Click on "Earth Science" and "Rock Types." Can you tell which types of rock below are which?

1 2 3 4

A) Shale   C) Limestone
B) Sandstone D) Gneiss

Answers 1) D, 2) A, 3) B, 4) C

Other Outdoor Adventures

There are many outdoor adventures similar to rock climbing. Some of these are bouldering, scrambling, ice climbing, and spelunking.

Bouldering

Bouldering is climbing rocks that are close to the ground, without ropes or harnesses. A bouldering wall is short, and climbers can fall to the ground safely. Mats are often placed on the ground below the wall to cushion falls. Climbers learn to fall feet first to avoid landing on their back, neck, or head. Bouldering is a good way to practice new climbing moves. Climbers can try more difficult moves on a short bouldering wall without becoming tired.

Scrambling

Scrambling is a type of climbing that does not use ropes or special gear. Scrambling uses both hands and feet to "scramble" over difficult and steep terrain while hiking. Scrambling can be a dangerous sport. Only experienced hikers should attempt it.
In recent years, this type of climbing has become common. Many guide books have been written about scrambling routes.

Ice climbing

Ice climbing is a challenging sport that has been practiced since the late 1800s. People can ice climb any place there is a frozen waterfall or large, steep piece of ice. Ice climbers use rock climbing gear, plus ice axes and crampons. Ice axes are specially designed to chop into the ice, creating handholds. Crampons are sharp metal spikes that attach to shoes. They allow a climber to step onto the ice without slipping.

get CONNECTED

Check out cave puzzles, experiments, quizzes, and art projects at www.cavetours.com. Click on "Kids Pages."

Spelunking

Spelunking is climbing in caves. Spelunkers explore underground worlds that are not often seen by people. Spelunking is similar to rock climbing. Spelunkers need rock climbing gear. They also need flashlights so they can see in dark places. Often, spelunkers attach the flashlight to their helmet.

Rock Climbing Around the World

ARCTIC
OCEAN

NORTH
AMERICA

PACIFIC
OCEAN

YOSEMITE VALLEY, UNITED STATES

Yosemite Valley in California is known for its huge granite walls. **Glaciers** formed the walls millions of years ago. The best-known rock wall for climbing in Yosemite is El Capitan. It is a 3,000-foot (914-m) sheet of granite. All the routes up El Capitan are difficult. Only expert climbers should try them. One of the routes, El Nino, is graded 5.13c and is 2,000 feet (609 m) high.

SOUTH
AMERICA

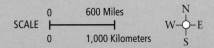

SCALE

0   600 Miles

0   1,000 Kilometers

N
W—E
S

There are many rock climbing sites all over the world. Some climbers prefer a certain type of rock. Others might choose a place for its scenery. The following climbing ranges are some of the most beautiful and challenging rock climbing sites in the world.

ARCTIC OCEAN

ARCTIC OCEAN

THE DOLOMITES, ITALY

The Dolomites are a group of limestone mountains in northeast Italy. The Dolomites have steep walls and tower-shaped rock formations. There are many routes for climbers of all skill levels. A unique feature of the Dolomites are the Via Ferratas. The Via Ferratas are cable walkways and ladders. They lead to places that cannot be reached by traditional climbing.

ASIA

EUROPE

PHRA NANG PENINSULA, THAILAND

Phra Nang **Peninsula** in Krabi is often described as a paradise for climbers. Its stunning limestone walls overhang a blue-green sea. The walls are covered in stalactites. Stalactites are pillars of limestone that look like icicles. They create interesting handholds and footholds. Phra Nang has hundreds of routes for both beginners and experts.

PACIFIC OCEAN

AFRICA

INDIAN OCEAN

MOUNT ARAPILES, AUSTRALIA

Mount Arapiles in Victoria is one of the world's best-known rock climbing sites. The mountain itself is a bright, flame-orange sandstone commonly seen throughout Australia. Arapiles is close to the city of Melbourne and easy to reach by car. The area usually has good weather and offers many routes for all levels of climbers.

AUSTRALIA

Join the Club

The Union Internationale des Associations d'Alpinisme (UIAA) was formed in 1932 in Chamoix, France. People from 18 countries started the organization. They wanted to promote safe climbing. They also wanted to help **preserve** mountain environments.

The UIAA urges climbers to protect the environment. Climbers can use environmentally friendly anchors that do not damage rock. Chocks are anchors that are wedged into cracks. They are removed after they are used. Many climbers now use chocks instead of bolts. Bolts are hammered into the rock. They chip and crack the rock. Bolts are left in the rock after being used.

The UIAA hosts some of the biggest rock climbing competitions in the world. They are the World Cup and the World Championship. The UIAA also hosts youth events.

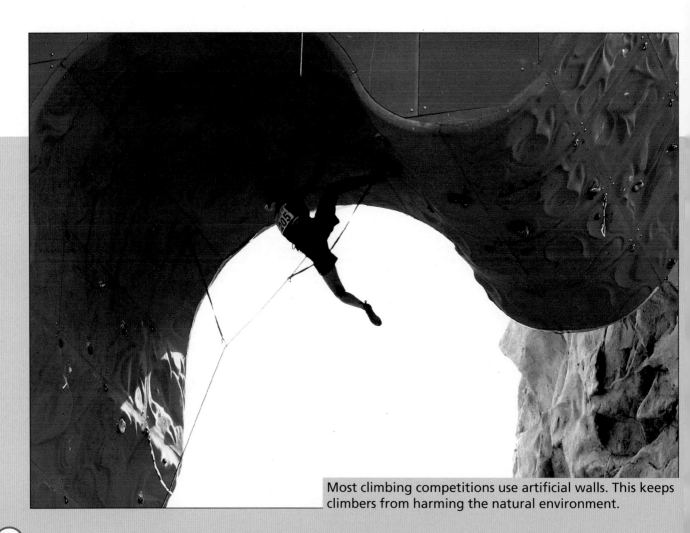

Most climbing competitions use artificial walls. This keeps climbers from harming the natural environment.

Rock climbing is also part of the World Games. The World Games are an 11-day sports event. Athletes from around the globe compete in more than 30 sports. Rock climbing events include bouldering and speed climbing.

Other activities are held all over the world. Climbing gyms have artificial walls. They offer lessons for people to learn the basics or build their climbing skills. Gyms also host local competitions.

get CONNECTED

To join the UIAA, visit http://ifsc-climbing.org. To learn about rock climbing events, and to see photos, visit http://climbing.com.

Healthy Habits

Rock climbers need to be healthy and fit. Eating well-balanced meals will help improve climbers' fitness. They will have more energy for long climbs and difficult moves. A balanced meal can include fruits, vegetables, dairy, grains, and protein.

Staying hydrated is also important to climbers' health. Climbers can do this by drinking plenty of water. People who participate in any kind of sport need to drink extra water. This is because their body loses water when they sweat.

Climbers also need strong arm and leg muscles to support their body weight for long periods of time. Many people train for climbing by running, hiking, and biking.

A sandwich made with chicken, tomatoes, lettuce, and whole grain bread, served with a piece of fruit and a glass of milk, is a good example of a well-balanced meal.

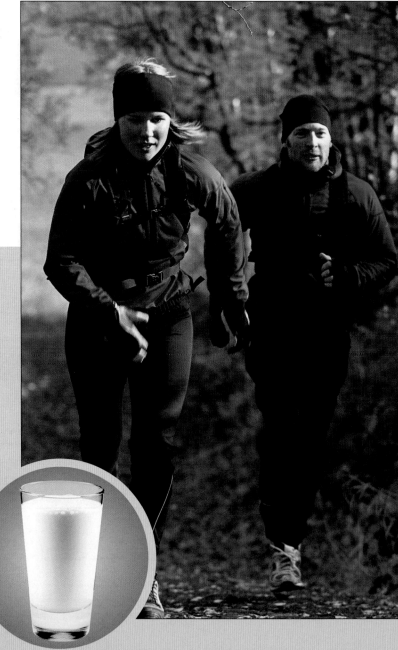

Milk is a good source of calcium. Calcium helps keep bones strong.

Climbers need to be flexible. This means they must be able to bend easily without breaking any bones or tearing any muscles. Climbers often stretch their body into strange positions to reach handholds and footholds in the rock. Yoga helps increase flexibility. Yoga uses different body positions and poses to teach balance. It is also a good way to learn how to control breathing. This is important because climbers must remain calm and keep their breathing steady.

Many gyms offer classes that teach yoga.

YOGA EXERCISE

- Stand straight up with your shoulders back and your arms hanging at your sides.

- Bend your right knee, and lift your right leg off the ground.

- Place the bottom of your right foot on the inside of your left calf or thigh.

- When you are ready, lift your arms straight above your head with your palms touching. Make sure to keep your shoulders down and relaxed.

- Hold the pose for 15 seconds.

- Release the pose, and switch sides.

Brain Teasers

Test your rock climbing knowledge by trying to answer these brain teasers.

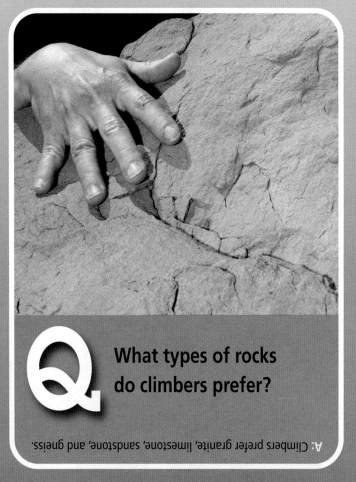

Q What types of rocks do climbers prefer?

A: Climbers prefer granite, limestone, sandstone, and gneiss.

Q What device can slow or stop a rope?

A: A belay device will slow or stop a rope.

Q What is a carabiner?

A: A carabiner is a metal loop with an opening that locks. It is used to connect pieces of climbing equipment.

Q. Why do most climbing competitions use artificial walls?

A: Climbing competitions use artificial walls to protect the natural environment.

Q. When do climbers smear?

A: Climbers smear when there is no ledge to grab on to or stand on.

Q. How do climbers avoid altitude sickness?

A: Climbers spend time at high altitudes to avoid sickness. They can also bring along bottled oxygen.

Glossary

absorb: soak up

altitude: height in relation to sea level

artificial: made by people; not natural

ascend: to climb upwards

compass: a tool, which uses a magnetic needle pointing north, used to determine direction

extreme sport: dangerous physical activity

glaciers: large bodies of ice

harnesses: straps fastened to a person's body

hypothermia: a dangerous loss of body heat caused by extremely cold weather

peninsula: a piece of land nearly surrounded by water or sticking out into the water

preserve: to keep something in its original state

rating: a grade or rank

route: the upward path a climber follows

vegetation: plant life

Index